Praise for *Applied Wisdom for the Nonprofit Sector*

"We're sharing this booklet with our nonprofit membership and incorporating it into our staff and board training program curriculums. It's useful for agencies of all sizes and domains."

— **Larissa Robideaux**
Executive Director, Center for Excellence in Nonprofits

"As a high-tech industry CEO and board chair, I strongly endorsed Jim's basic principles for success in the business world. Now, retired and a nonprofit board chair, I see how effective his principles apply to nonprofits as well as to donors. They work and make a difference."

— **Dave House**
Retired CEO, Bay Networks and Board Chair, Silicon Valley Education Foundation

"Foundation trustees need help effectively allocating their funding. This booklet offers countless insights for those investing in nonprofits as well as the nonprofits themselves. Jim's combined experience as a successful businessman, nonprofit board leader and philanthropist offers deep understanding from all three worlds."

— **Matson Sewell**
Co-trustee and Grants Manager, Arata Brothers Trust

"A compact booklet with timely and sound wisdom, truth and practical advice, including useful, provocative questions. I've distributed the booklet to my 100 senior leaders and my board. Jim has already had a significant impact on our thinking and leadership."

— **Albert L. Reyes, DMin, Ph.D.**
President and CEO, Buckner International

"This booklet delivers on its promise. This easy-to-read but powerful collection of leadership principles provides real value, not just for chief executives, but for the board members who lead with them. The practical wisdom, and especially the collection of questions for board discussion, are excellent resources for any nonprofit board committed to truly advancing their nonprofit's mission."

— **Mary Hiland, Ph.D.**
Nonprofit Governance Consultant

Visit AppliedWisdomforNonprofits.org
to download this booklet in print and audio formats,
order additional print copies,
and access learning tools and resources.

Applied Wisdom

FOR THE

NONPROFIT

SECTOR

Eight Practical Insights for Leaders

JAMES C. MORGAN

Second Edition

Chandler Jordan Publishing

Acknowledgments

I would like to thank everyone who contributed to the success of *Applied Wisdom for the Nonprofit Sector*. The whole team at the Morgan Family Foundation, Linda Verhulp, Lisa Downey, Mary Yang Smith, and Mara Yarp; as well as Diane Parnes, Thad McIlroy, Jim McDonough, Becky Morgan, Joe Pon, Ethan Hawkes and Joan O'C. Hamilton.

Published and distributed by Chandler Jordan Publishing, Los Altos, CA

ISBN (paperback): 978-0-9983292-7-7
ISBN (PDF): 978-0-9983292-8-4
ISBN (ebook): 978-0-9983292-9-1

Adapted from *Applied Wisdom: Bad News Is Good News and Other Insights That Can Help Anyone Be a Better Manager* by James C. Morgan and Joan O'C. Hamilton.

Project Director & Content Development: Diane Parnes, *EVOLUTIONARY* Philanthropy & Nonprofit Services

Publication and Editorial Consultant: Thad McIlroy, The Future of Publishing

Digital Strategy and Website: Jim McDonough

Cover and interior page design by Geoff Ahmann, AKA – Ahmann Kadlec Associates

Ebook production by Kevin Callaghan, BNGO Books

Copyediting by Meri Furnari

Printed in the United States by McNaughton & Gunn

AppliedWisdomforNonprofits.org

CONTENTS

Foreword by Diane Parnes

Congratulations — you are about to be mentored by one of Silicon Valley's most respected and admired leaders, Jim Morgan. Jim is revered for his character, humility and integrity, people-oriented management style, and commitment to the community.

Jim describes his calling as helping to maximize the potential of individuals and organizations. His time-tested business insights, concisely distilled in *Applied Wisdom for the Nonprofit Sector*, offer practical ways for anyone to become a more effective leader. Throughout my 30 years' experience serving as a chief executive of nonprofits and grantmaking institutions, one thing stands out clearly: investing in strong leadership and management is key to achieving outstanding organizational results.

With the gift of Jim's booklet, nonprofit and philanthropic professionals and their boards will learn that a deliberate focus on people and culture, short- and long-term planning, and efficient implementation of decisions, will significantly improve their effectiveness. Donors will learn how to assess the qualities of high-performing nonprofits, and, ideally, emulate Jim's example of providing unrestricted, operating dollars to meet nonprofits' greatest needs.

Let's all "wise up" and actively apply Jim's insights to support a sector that's inclusive, vibrant and effective, and create the most value for the beneficiaries of our work.

In community spirit,

Diane Parnes
Founder & CEO
EVOLUTIONARY Philanthropy & Nonprofit Services

A Note from Jim Morgan

I began working at our family business, Morgan & Sons Canning, at a young age. As I look back, I realize how fortunate I was that my father and grandfather set an example about how to be ethical and effective in business. They taught me about managing people and the importance of treating everyone with respect.

I got a great education at Cornell University, then served two meaningful years in the U.S. Army, followed by several years in high-tech business and investing. In 1976 I joined Applied Materials, a semiconductor equipment manufacturer, and ran it for nearly three decades. The company was near bankruptcy when I joined; when I retired in 2003, Applied Materials was a multi-billion-dollar global leader employing over 15,000 people in 18 countries. Since that time, I've committed myself to nonprofit board service and philanthropic work.

Developing My Management Insights

Learning about leadership and management has been a lifelong passion. In the process, I've discovered many valuable lessons that have impacted my professional career, community work, and personal life. I realized how my early experiences in the cannery connected to other challenges and opportunities in business; many of those experiences became the basis of ideas that I would talk about on the job. At some point, members of my Applied Materials team started calling them "Morganisms."

In my 2016 autobiography *Applied Wisdom: Bad News Is Good News If You Do Something About It*, I documented over 100 of these Morganisms. Some of my friends commented that they have benefited from using the Morganisms in their personal lives. I've used them as a management tool when advising executives, staff, and boards of global and local nonprofits. They work regardless of the size or domain of an organization. The concepts have become a shared language, increasing understanding and trust among and between staff and board and even donors. And I rely on them when I consider where to volunteer and where to give money.

For this booklet, I've focused on eight simple insights that have consistently delivered the best results. I hope that these can help support the nonprofit sector in three specific ways.

First, that they can help individuals develop their abilities as leaders and managers; and make them more effective and increase their productivity.

Second, that they can help organizations strengthen the capacity and adaptability of their diverse staff and board teams to lead them through complexity and change.

Finally, that they can help donors understand how unrestricted dollars are vital to achieving an organization's strategic goals and mission.

Success Requires Effective Leadership

It's been said that the one constant in life is change. But the basic demands and challenges of management have not changed much since my days in the cannery. Running an organization demands leadership and management. While closely related, these are not the same nor are they interchangeable. As Peter Drucker, the leader of modern management theory, once proclaimed, "Management is doing things right; leadership is doing the right things."

All organizations face challenges in managing people. The best managers empower their people and help them maximize their potential. Unlocking and encouraging excellence in others has been the most satisfying aspect of my career. I believe that every person, regardless of education, training, or current position, is capable of improving their leadership and management skills, whether in a global company or a nonprofit filled with passion but limited in resources.

To your success....

Jim Morgan
Chair, Morgan Family Foundation
Co-Founder, The Northern Sierra Partnership
Chairman Emeritus, Applied Materials, Inc.

How to Use this Booklet

There are eight chapters in this booklet, each built around my management insights and focused on the three pillars of a successful organization — culture, planning, and implementation. But the insights don't only apply to those realms. They can be used across a broad spectrum of organizational practices. I've included some personal stories and examples to reinforce how these ideas apply in different settings.

To gain the most value from this booklet, let me suggest a few ways to approach the material.

While you can open the booklet to any insight that piques your interest, I would encourage you to read the entire booklet from start to finish. It will only take 20 to 30 minutes — perfect for a short train commute or a flight. Each time you reread the booklet you'll obtain more from it. If you prefer listening to the text while taking a walk or driving, go to **AppliedWisdomforNonprofits.org** where you can download the audiobook. You might consider reading the booklet and then also listening to it as a way to deepen your understanding of the concepts.

Reflecting on Applied Wisdom

After your initial read (or listen), think about a current situation where one of the insights may be helpful. Can you dialogue about the management concept at your next staff or board meeting or share it in conversation with friends?

Feel free to jump around in the booklet, referring to a particular insight and then consciously applying it to different situations — personal as well as work-related. The more you think and act on them, the more familiar and comfortable they will become.

To help stimulate your thinking, at the end of each chapter you will find a set of "Conversation Starters" for chief executives, staff team members, board members, individual donors, and institutional philanthropies. While you may identify with just one or two roles, I encourage you to read the full set of prompts to gain broader and more diverse perspectives about how others might think about the insights.

Let's dig in….

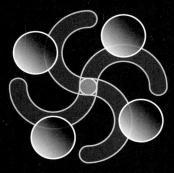

1

Cultivating Culture

Culture matters. It's a core organizational asset.

The role of leadership is to build a strong organizational culture based on a nonprofit's purpose, mission, vision, and values. You want people at every level of your enterprise to have a clear sense of its purpose as well as its immediate and long-term goals, and to feel a sense of belonging and respect. An exceptional culture will attract great employees and volunteers, board members, and supportive donors who can propel your mission forward.

A Values-Based Culture

To lead a nonprofit through changing times, remember why the organization exists and what it stands for. Be conscious of the culture that you want and use every opportunity to create and nurture it.

Culture is built upon your nonprofit's values. Your staff and board must articulate and embrace those values. If you don't develop processes collaboratively by inviting input from all stakeholders, your culture may become plagued by simmering resentments. Many unproductive attitudes can infect an organization that does not pay close attention to its mission, vision, and values. A culture that promotes and rewards respect and trust will be healthy and productive.

To build an energetic environment and culture, you have to be explicit about the behaviors that you value. Reward the behaviors that reinforce the culture you're striving for, aligned with policies and practices. Seek a clear understanding of why staff and volunteers stay or why they leave the organization; and what this might say about your operation.

Your constituents' needs change, staff and boards come and go, new tools emerge, and economies shift. In a dynamic work environment, you will never be "done" putting management systems and processes into effect. But through it all, the quality of the workplace experience is defined by the consistency of the values that you consciously cultivate and communicate.

Your culture is also visible externally to all of your constituents, volunteers, donors, patrons, and government contract funders. Clearly communicating and promoting your nonprofit's impact and being transparent about the effective stewardship of resources serve as inspiration for your supporters to engage with, contribute to, and advocate for your mission.

I like to think that at Applied Materials we hired the right people and listened to them carefully. We supported their efforts with the required resources and encouragement, even in tough, cyclical times. In return, all of those elements produced a culture where work was valued and where people worked hard for success.

When things are going well, it's easy to take your culture for granted. When things aren't going well, many managers will focus on some quality that they believe is deficient. They might suddenly decide, "we need to change the culture" or "we need to bring in a consultant." Catchy slogans are developed and printed on mugs and t-shirts, an offsite is scheduled, and the topic of "culture" is suddenly on the agenda of every meeting.

But you will never change an organization's culture just by telling employees that the culture needs to change. An offsite discussion might help you reach agreement about what is out of alignment, but it won't create permanent change. You must do something, take deliberate action. Make real changes and communicate them — not just once, but repeatedly and consistently.

If you want to build a certain kind of culture, or you want to rebuild a failing culture, you need the right structure, processes, and people. Analyze your operations for gaps or misalignment. Make sure your managers are accountable for prioritizing change, and that your team is as skilled and focused as possible. If you do these things properly, your culture will change over time. It's every team member's job to "walk the talk" and commit to building a great enterprise.

Tone at the Top

A board's responsibility includes the oversight of a healthy internal culture. While your board has limited exposure to your nonprofit's day-to-day operation, it must ensure that the chief executive is articulating the organization's values and cultivating culture at every level.

Boards should also be aligned with the values of the organization. When board members behave courteously and respectfully toward each other and management, they set an example for staff to emulate. The culture of the board is part of the "tone at the top."

As it's so often said, culture eats strategy for breakfast. Culture matters. It's your core organizational asset and establishes whether your nonprofit is just good — or if it becomes great.

Conversation Starters

For Chief Executives

1. How do your actions and behaviors help to cultivate your desired culture? What three actions or behaviors can you commit to improving?

2. What processes do you have in place to seek feedback about your culture from all stakeholders? How do you address any misalignments between the real and perceived culture of your organization?

For Staff Team Members

1. Describe your nonprofit's purpose and values; how do your daily actions and behaviors align with those values? What could help you bring them into greater alignment?

2. In what ways does your workplace reflect a healthy culture? (In what ways does it not?) What three ideas do you have that could strengthen your organization's culture?

For Board Members

1. How does the board ensure that the chief executive is cultivating a healthy culture?

2. Thinking about the board's decision-making processes, actions and behaviors, how would you describe the culture of your board? How well does the board's culture align with the organization's broader culture and values?

For Individual Donors

1. What can you tell about an organization's culture and values from looking at its website, annual report, promotional materials or donation appeals?

2. What impact might an organization's culture have on its ability to deliver on its mission?

For Institutional Philanthropies

1. To what degree do the values of your grantees align with your institution's values? How could greater alignment benefit both you and your grantees?

2. How do you assess a nonprofit's culture? Why might it be important for you to consider that culture as part of your due diligence process?

2

Respect and Trust Your People

**Respecting and trusting your people
is the foundation of all good management.**

To successfully lead you must paint a vision of where your nonprofit is headed and what behaviors and attitudes you will value on the journey. You need to establish the qualities of your leadership and the character of the organization. Your tone and behavior should show regard for every employee's strengths, contributions, and cultural background, as well as their health, workplace comfort, and psychological safety. If you are disrespectful of your employees or you disregard their dignity, you undermine trust.

As a leader, you are constantly being evaluated by your team as to whether you treat people with respect and trust. You hire the best people you can and then you trust them to use their judgment to do the right thing. If you don't respect and trust an employee, then you should question why they are still working for you.

Cultivate a supportive organizational culture that moves your nonprofit toward its goals while promoting a respectful workplace where people can contribute their best. Trust is born of respect.

Caring and Collaboration

A key element of respect is encouraging personal discipline and healthy habits so that you and your teams have the stamina and energy to enjoy long-term success. First, take care of your health and fitness. Pay attention to the physical dimensions of your workspace. I encourage people to wear comfortable shoes to work so that they can periodically get up and take a walking break. Moving around during the day keeps the mind sharp and the body relaxed. Establish policies that promote a reasonable work-life balance for employees. Prioritizing and scheduling time for personal relationships, family life, and hobbies is equally important for your mental and emotional health and will help you balance your life and perform better.

Encourage other types of caring behaviors within the organization. Look around and observe how your staff team members interact and care for one another. It's important to prioritize building human connections — they are an important key to success and fundamental to forming trusting relationships. Connections start with conversations. I've often scheduled "walking meetings" with people I need to speak to one-on-one. It pays dividends to plan offsite meetings where your staff can socialize and build rapport, and where boards can engage in deeper generative discussions.

Building positive relations between your people — staff and board — also helps develop your team's ability to work together better. I encourage people to approach all teamwork with a collaborative mindset, where you treat your partner's success as equal to your own. That applies to internal relationships, external partnerships, and donors.

Hire Deliberately

An organization committed to excellence deliberately focuses on building strong teams. It's critical to identify and recruit a diversity of people who share a commitment to your mission and are willing to learn and adapt as your nonprofit's needs change. Hire for purpose and potential first, for skills second. Before making an employment offer, listen for at least two potential shortcomings that you are willing to live with.

Hiring high-caliber people is always the aim; competence is not sufficient. By high-caliber, I mean people who are resilient, intelligent, and problem solvers. You'll benefit from assembling a diverse and inclusive team with complementary skills and a range of functional backgrounds.

Employee Growth and Satisfaction

Organizations benefit greatly by creating a culture of continuous learning. Staff need professional development opportunities to improve their skills and to gain new ideas. Leaders should communicate and reinforce the value of ongoing education and training opportunities to their staff so that employees take all learning programs seriously. The more employees develop and have the opportunity to contribute to your nonprofit in new ways, the more likely they are to be happy and loyal while working on behalf of your mission.

Financial independence and success are major motivators in life. And, ideally, nonprofit professionals should be able to do well while pursuing the larger goal of doing good. Since nonprofits operate on lean budgets, employee compensation is always a delicate subject. I often hear how employees are overworked and underpaid, and that turnover is high, particularly for fundraising professionals. The chief executive and board should prioritize offering respectable wages and benefits and educate donors on how general operating funds enable the organization to attract and retain excellent people.

Conversation Starters

For Chief Executives

1. How does your organization demonstrate respect for the strengths, contributions, and cultural backgrounds of your employees? How do your policies support their health, workplace comfort, and psychological safety?

2. How do your organization's hiring, promotion, and compensation practices demonstrate respect for your people? How do you ensure that you are integrating diversity, equity, and inclusion into your organization?

For Staff Team Members

1. In what ways does your chief executive model respect and trust? What could they improve?

2. How does your team demonstrate caring, listening, and working collaboratively? What are some opportunities for improvement?

For Board Members

1. What are three ways your board could work more collaboratively as a team and in partnership with your chief executive?

2. How, in the organization's strategic plan and budget, is the board prioritizing equitable compensation and benefits and also encouraging professional growth for all employees?

For Individual Donors

1. How can you assess whether a nonprofit respects and trusts its people and community stakeholders when planning and executing on its mission?

2. How can a nonprofit demonstrate respect and trust to its donors?

For Institutional Philanthropies

1. In what ways do your grantmaking practices communicate respect and trust to your grant applicants? How could you deepen those further?

2. How well does your current funding support grantees in providing respectable wages and benefits, investing in leadership skill development, and strengthening staff and board diversity, equity and inclusion? How could new or increased funding further encourage your grantees to deliver in these areas?

Bad News is Good News

Always listen for and even seek out signs of trouble.
Bad news is good news if you do something about it.

Nonprofits are in the business of tackling tough challenges — addressing poverty, improving education, and protecting the planet. The passionate, smart, and good-hearted people who work in the sector are filled with optimism. This can make it uncomfortable for them to acknowledge a looming crisis. But to be successful, a leader must master the ability to perceive, acknowledge, and respond to threats as well as opportunities.

At Applied Materials, we saw bad news as an opportunity for innovation or a strategic shift. We had a saying: "Good news is no news. No news is bad news. And bad news is good news — if you do something about it."

Of course, it's important to celebrate successes. But only up to a point. You can't bury problems or refuse to address negative issues. Do you welcome early warnings or are you ignoring them?

Porpoising

I called my bad news early detection system "porpoising." Think about a porpoise, repeatedly diving deep into the ocean and then rising to the surface; gathering information at all levels. As a manager, you should periodically "porpoise" beyond your direct reports to talk to diverse groups of people at every level in your nonprofit.

Porpoising is designed to unearth valuable information, whether in the short term or for the long haul. Porpoising expresses a culture of observant listening — and enables you to "hear" sounds of trouble before you learn about it through official channels. Seek to understand by visiting teams and asking simple questions: What is going on here? Is the organization in your way? Why are deadlines slipping? What would you do to fix that? The key is to listen respectfully so that your employees are comfortable sharing what's going on and giving you actionable information. To maintain that trust you will need to act on the information given. Be present and visible. I would sometimes take a sack lunch and eat with employees or drop in and sit in the back row of a meeting to observe, listen, and learn.

Also, ask board members to speak up when they see problems developing. You can even porpoise with other nonprofits, community stakeholders, individual donors, and grantmakers to gain valuable insights and to leverage their knowledge and expertise.

But what if there's no news or if no one has news to report? Without feedback, even top leaders have trouble assessing what's going on. I've learned that no news can be a sign of bad news — it may mean people or things are not moving forward. There are always problems or issues of concern to address. If things are quiet for too long, it's time to porpoise and listen carefully. You'll always find something good or bad. You just need to know which is which.

And if it's bad news? Bad news is good news because it gives you a chance to address problems before they spiral out of control.

Building a culture that embraces values such as "bad news is good news" doesn't happen overnight. And it needs to be reinforced by rewarding early detection. Everyone within your organization should encourage frank discussions of bad news. You must identify problems and then emphasize finding solutions, rather than assigning blame. Celebrate the solutions! Bad news is good news if you do something about it.

Bad News is Essential for Boards

Chief executives understandably like to highlight their successes to their board. But openly sharing bad news is an effective method for building mutual respect and trust. While it may be difficult at first, sharing bad news will help form a strong partnership with your board, important for bad times.

Inviting board member questions and listening to their feedback enables you to understand their concerns and to have an opportunity to learn from them. I like to say — speak once, listen twice.

By including bad news as part of board meetings, the chief executive, senior staff, and the board can explore ideas and learn together. You need to hash out what isn't working or what's keeping your top executive up late at night. In creating a greater shared understanding, your board can help to improve your nonprofit's productivity and performance. By brainstorming new paths of opportunity together you will build an organization that you can all be proud of.

Conversation Starters

For Chief Executives

1. In what ways do you currently "porpoise" within your organization, making sure that you're hearing from all departments at all levels? How have you made staff comfortable with sharing bad news when you porpoise?

2. How do you ensure that bad news is a focus at every board meeting? How do you integrate the board's advice and counsel into your actions and communicate outcomes back to the board?

For Staff Team Members

1. How comfortable are you sharing bad news with your manager? In what ways do you see porpoising as being different from being micro-managed?

2. How do you and your colleagues work together to turn bad news into good news? What practices could strengthen your teamwork even more?

For Board Members

1. At board meetings, what process is in place to enable the chief executive and senior staff to comfortably discuss bad news and seek out constructive advice? How will meeting agendas shift to accommodate these discussions?

2. How does feedback from clients, employees, key stakeholders and donors influence the board's planning and implementation work?

For Individual Donors

1. How do you go about "porpoising" to learn about a nonprofit before making a donation or deciding to volunteer?

2. How might hearing a bad news story about the nonprofit sector impact your behavior as a donor?

For Institutional Philanthropies

1. How do you "porpoise" with grant applicants when conducting due diligence and in-person site visits?

2. How do you encourage grantees to share bad news with you? How does bad news from grantees impact your funding commitments?

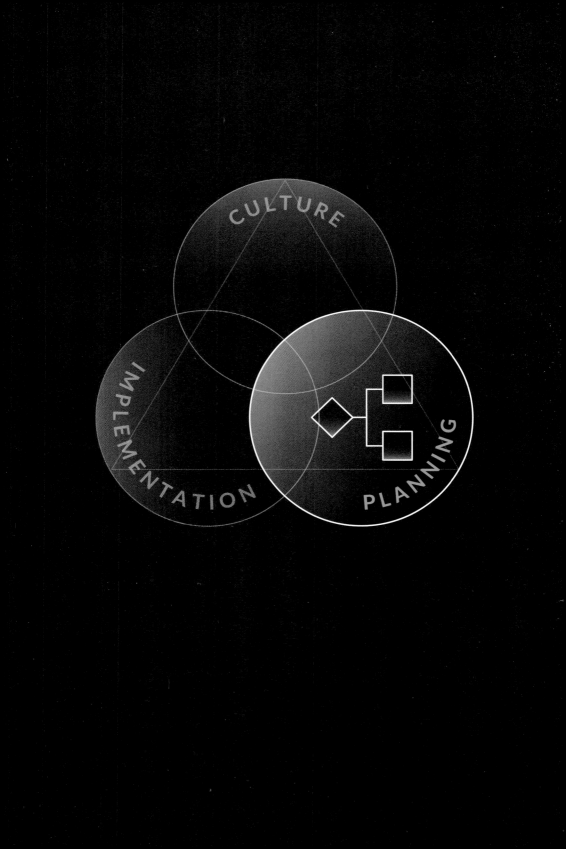

CULTURE

IMPLEMENTATION

PLANNING

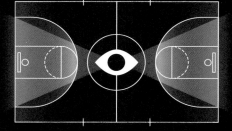

Develop Court Sense

Develop "court sense" to see everything that's happening around you, and to rapidly adjust to changes.

I've always liked basketball because it is an intense and fluid game. There's no standing around waiting for a pitch or lining up and waiting for a snap. While you have a game plan, you have to adjust on the fly. You study your opponents' behavior and focus on seizing opportunities as they arise. Playing basketball helped give me "court sense," an ability to pay attention to and manage more than one thing going on, and to adjust to fast-changing variables to predict where the next opening or opportunity might be.

Court sense is the alert, action-oriented posture that sports like basketball demand for success. But it's not just for sports. When our kids were young, our family did quite a bit of river rafting in Northern California. My daughter enjoyed it so much that she became a weekend guide and developed her version of court sense.

As a rafting guide, you have to have skill, but you also have to pay attention to other factors, like the skill-level of your guests, the weather, the water current, and hazards like rocks or a log that can suddenly appear. You have a plan, but you also have to paddle down the river with your head up and your eyes open. You can't ignore a sign of danger or a problem that might sink the raft. You have to develop confidence and adjust quickly when conditions change. As the guide, you pilot the boat; and the better your court sense, the better the outcome.

Where does your court sense come from?

Court Sense for Nonprofits

In the nonprofit sector, "court sense" means understanding the environment that impacts your organization. You can't hone your court sense in a vacuum — or an echo chamber. It's valuable to take time regularly to step out of your comfort zone, and out of the weeds of daily tasks and pressing issues. A disciplined way to put your court sense into play is through annual and multi-year planning cycles.

Your job is to look up, look forward, and look around. Be ready to react to changing conditions and threats, and to identify new opportunities to innovate and to take risks. To thrive in a complex world, you can't just slog forward every day checking off boxes in a linear fashion. You have to anticipate problems, process new information, and adjust your strategy. This is systems thinking. And systems thinking requires court sense.

Driving Forces

In thinking about the long-term direction of your nonprofit, it's critical to assess driving forces. Driving forces include demographic shifts like the rise of millennials, issues surrounding equity, diversity, and inclusion, and the global interest in reducing reliance on fossil fuels. Micro driving forces can be unique, possibly fleeting opportunities, such as a community partner's strategic program shift, changes in tax law, or a lapse in government funding.

A good leader is constantly looking for what is likely to impact the organization's future. Get used to assessing driving forces early and often. Your ability to perceive and incorporate them into your thinking will improve over time. Reflect on how you, your board, and staff are strategically positioning your organization to take advantage of change. Systematically seek client feedback and analyze program evaluation data to inform your thinking. Every significant decision should assess relevant driving forces, both short-term and long-term.

While strategic decision-making always includes risk, developing your court sense and regularly assessing trends will help shape your instincts and reflexes. It will inform the way you lead and how your people work, make decisions, deliver services, and relate to clients and donors.

The Inspirational Why

To be an effective manager, you need to be sensitive to how organizational change affects your employees. Rapid ups and downs are rough on people and create tension. Employees can fall into predictable patterns where they might deny what's going on, become discouraged, or resist change. A common mistake is to ignore the tension and just keep adding more responsibilities to people who are already working very hard. But your employees' energy and commitment are vital. By listening to your staff and engaging in open, honest conversations, you can build bridges of understanding and enhance workplace morale.

Even amid disruption, always focus on your nonprofit's goals and values to keep your team's focus on the inspirational why of your work — the reason your organization exists.

Conversation Starters

For Chief Executives

1. How do you factor driving forces into your organization's annual and multi-year planning cycles? When you detect changing conditions, how do you adjust your strategies and find ways to move forward?

2. What steps have you taken to prepare your staff to respond to rapidly changing external conditions and trends? What do you do to pay attention to employees' needs during times of change?

For Staff Team Members

1. How does using your "court sense" inform the way that you work, make decisions, deliver services, and relate to clients and donors?

2. Think of a time when you or your organization had to make a quick adjustment. What did that experience teach you? What, if anything, would you differently next time?

For Board Members

1. What current significant trends and driving forces provide the organization with opportunities for growth and change?

2. How can you support the chief executive and staff through times of rapid change to confront the challenge of work overload and the risk of burn out?

For Individual Donors

1. How do you use your "court sense" when considering where you might make a donation or volunteer?

2. How do driving forces in our world shape your philanthropic interests? How do they impact where you decide to direct your donations or to volunteer your time?

For Institutional Philanthropies

1. How does your "court sense" inform your grantmaking?

2. How do driving forces in our world shape your giving strategies, priorities and approach?

The Whole Job

Commit to doing "the whole job."
Investing in organizational capacity
contributes to excellence and impact.

When I joined The Nature Conservancy (TNC) Asia Pacific Council, one of my priorities was to convey to our teams the concept of "the whole job." Environmental expertise and developing creative solutions to preserve the ecosystem were the main focus. But, in order to do "the whole job," it is also important to develop strength in finance, fundraising, marketing, and hiring.

Your nonprofit has specific functions and processes, as well as regulations it must follow. You spend and control cash, acquire facilities and equipment, hire and train a diverse team, manage information and much more. Sometimes you can fill gaps and create efficiencies by leveraging volunteer expertise, seeking opportunities for collaboration, or sharing back-office operations. All are effective ways to strengthen your nonprofit while reducing administrative costs. A weakness in any operational area can negate successes in others. Over time, without all the parts functioning well, the entire organization will suffer. Commit to doing "the whole job."

Face the Elevator Door

Change is the medium of opportunity. At Applied Materials, my team developed the concept to "face the elevator door." With shifting economic cycles, things happen that can help or hurt an organization. You need to prepare yourself to capitalize on an opportunity (the elevator door opening) regardless of where your nonprofit may be in its lifecycle or in implementing its strategic plan. As a leader you need to be out front, thinking ahead of the game. By staying attuned to the macroeconomic forces that can impact your revenue, you'll be ready to move when the momentum shifts, the door closes, and the elevator changes direction.

Investing in people and infrastructure is essential. When revenues are strong, control your spending and aim to build a cash reserve that can cover three to six months of operating costs. When the economic climate changes, causing a downturn in earned revenue or charitable contributions, your organization will be well-positioned to meet urgent or emerging needs. Cash is king. Raise it when you can; don't wait until you need it. Always protect your downside.

Fundraising challenges add more volatility to the mix. Many major donors impose restrictions on their gifts and grants. This increases risk and can even cause harm.

Your nonprofit will prosper if you focus on finding and cultivating donors who share your vision. To attract multi-year gifts ensuring your sustainability, you'll need to show donors and grantmakers a multi-year strategic plan and budget to sustain and grow your organization's impact. I am always impressed when a nonprofit has an honest conversation with me about how unrestricted general operating support will best help them achieve their goals.

A Humble Approach to Giving

I've been deeply engaged in philanthropy for more than two decades and have had exposure to a wide variety of nonprofits through our family foundation. Friends and colleagues often ask me how I assess the effectiveness of a nonprofit. I share with them that I have the highest regard for organizations that have:

1. Strong leadership with a bold vision and a strong plan for implementation.

2. A clear mission that spells out what the organization seeks to accomplish and why it's important.

3. Transparency regarding finances, governance, program evaluation, outcomes, and impact.

4. Strong partnerships with donors, volunteers, other nonprofits, businesses, and government.

My wife Becky and I have encouraged our family, foundation staff, and fellow donors to apply those same principles in their philanthropic efforts or when considering where to volunteer or serve on a nonprofit board.

No matter the size or type of contribution, take a humble approach to giving. Trusting a nonprofit's leadership and contributing unrestricted dollars to support their whole mission is a sign of respect. While an organization's budget may have line items for people and infrastructure separate from program costs, they can't operate without both. Investing in leadership development — for both staff and board — is an impactful contribution to help sustain and grow an organization.

Both individual donors and institutional philanthropies must invest strategically, sufficiently, and over the long-term. Nonprofits and donors become a team when they think of doing "the whole job" together.

Conversation Starters

For Chief Executives

1. What staff and other capacity investments are needed for your organization to increase its impact? How do you educate your board and donors about essential infrastructure investments?

2. How do you prepare to capitalize on opportunity, thinking ahead of the game for your organization?

For Staff Team Members

1. What are you doing to help your organization face the elevator door?

2. How do you and your colleagues contribute to gaining donor support for doing "the whole job"?

For Board Members

1. How does the board support the chief executive and staff to be ready to capitalize on opportunity, the elevator door opening?

2. How well do the board's fundraising efforts support the organization's need to do "the whole job"? What are ways that you can strengthen your messaging to promote that concept?

For Individual Donors

1. What principles are important to you when considering where you make a donation or choose to volunteer?

2. Does your approach to giving demonstrate respect for and a commitment to the organization doing "the whole job"?

For Institutional Philanthropies

1. How can you engage in more open, honest conversations with nonprofits about their essential staff and infrastructure needs?

2. How can you educate your philanthropy's board about the importance of providing unrestricted funding for nonprofits so they can effectively do "the whole job"?

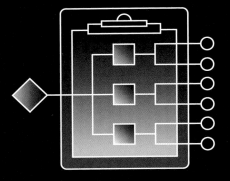

Prioritize and Focus

With limited time and resources,
it's essential to prioritize and then focus.

Organizational success is a marathon, not a sprint. Today, many individuals and nonprofits run at an unsustainable pace that is reactive, but not strategic. With limited time and resources, it's essential to set priorities and then focus on what's most important. As a leader, you must motivate everyone — staff and board — to march in the same direction and maintain focus. People have to trust the leader's vision and accept responsibility for helping make that vision a reality.

10% for Planning

Planning to implement a nonprofit's vision and strategy requires looking at both the short term and the long haul. I always urge staff teams to spend at least 10% percent of their time each week planning. Taking time to plan and confer creates a useful rhythm and routine. Stepping away from the daily grind challenges you to slow down, reflect, and adjust your plans as needed.

One of the practices I've always preached is what I call the "Rule of Three." You should always identify and focus on three priorities. Start each day reassessing and reaffirming them. Have a separate list of priorities for a day, week, month, three months, and up to a year. While most of us do many more things in a day, or a year, you need to budget your time so that your top priorities are always front and center.

"Priority management" is much more powerful than "time management." Make sure that all of your activities, each day, are moving you past short-term priorities and toward longer-term goals. You'll gain a feeling of control when you move away from being constantly in reactive mode. Don't let the urgent rob time from more important long-term priorities. Review your best ideas at least weekly, prioritize them, and think about when they can become actionable. Never treat long-term goals as something you plan to "get to" in a year.

Board Priorities

Nonprofit boards have three primary governance responsibilities. Priority one is setting strategic direction. Second is ensuring adequate financial and human resources. And third is providing oversight to fulfill the nonprofit's mission.

Part of a board's value is its ability to take the long view. Being a thought partner to the chief executive offers your nonprofit a broad range of perspectives. Recruiting a diverse board with a range of functional experiences and networks from different industries and among different stakeholder groups is more likely to produce a healthy mix of viewpoints, advice, and counsel.

Board work requires discipline. Using your organizational multi-year strategic plan and budget, the chief executive and the board chair should design an annual "conversation map" focused on what decisions need to be made and when. Meeting agendas should center more heavily on engaging in generative conversations to reflect, solve problems, and create meaning. Strategic and fiduciary issues also then need to be covered to monitor the nonprofit's agreed-upon goals, outcomes, and financial metrics.

Plan to Succeed

I served for nine years on the global board at The Nature Conservancy (TNC). Our governance committee focused on two key oversight functions. First, to drive better performance, we developed a strong planning process for conducting annual performance reviews for the chief executive as well as the board itself and individual board members. Reviews such as these are an opportunity to build trust and to keep people motivated and focused. A healthy process and conversation will recognize good work and discuss areas that can be strengthened. Throughout the year, you can promote a culture of listening and learning by providing ongoing coaching and offering constructive feedback.

Secondly, our governance committee developed succession plans for both the chief executive and the board officers, so that we were prepared for either an emergency or for a planned leadership transition. These plans became tools to help align our talent development with our future leadership needs. In this situation, my "Rule of Three" is to create a personal list of at least three people whom you think could be good additions to the staff and board teams, being attentive to your organization's commitment to diversity, equity, and inclusion.

Success comes from continually prioritizing and focusing on your goals. You must plan to succeed. And you must plan... to succeed!

Conversation Starters

For Chief Executives

1. What would enable you to devote 10% of your weekly schedule to short- and long-term planning? What would you eliminate from your current schedule?

2. How do you engage your board in serving as your thought partner? What do you do to ensure that they remain focused on their top three governance responsibilities?

For Staff Team Members

1. How do you go about setting your work priorities, both short-term and long-term? What are your top three priorities today and this week?

2. How can you create time in your weekly schedule to reflect on your priorities and adjust them as needed? How will you communicate any planning changes to your manager?

For Board Members

1. How do you establish your annual work plan and priorities? What training and education programs could strengthen new member onboarding and ongoing governance performance?

2. What processes are in place to provide the chief executive, individual board members, and the board collectively, with ongoing feedback and an annual performance assessment?

For Individual Donors

1. Before giving to a nonprofit, how can you gather information about its strategic plan and finances?

2. Does your giving tend to be more strategic or reactive? How might committing to multi-year giving be beneficial to the nonprofits you support?

For Institutional Philanthropies

1. How often do your board and staff refocus your grantmaking approach and priorities? How do you communicate these shifts to your grantees?

2. How can funding a nonprofit's board and staff development, strategic planning, and executive succession planning be wise investments?

7

Book It and Ship It

Planning is essential but success comes from the implementation of your ideas. "Book It and Ship It." Make a decision and manage the consequences.

One of the biggest challenges of leadership is moving ideas to action — implementation. I saw this when I had the opportunity to serve on the Board of The Nature Conservancy (TNC). I saw that a disproportionate amount of time was spent strategizing and reorganizing. In the process, I became known for using the phrase "book it and ship it."

Success is 90% Implementation

In the manufacturing business, "book it and ship it" means, "we're finished building this. Let's move on." It's a plea to get on to execution. I used it at TNC as a way of saying, "No more dithering. We've done our best here; now let's put the decision in motion and see what happens." If problems develop, you manage them. But kicking the can down the road over and over just saps energy. While time should be spent on organizing, strategizing, and planning, success comes from the implementation of ideas. Going from planning to doing requires courage and involves risk.

My experience is that you have to cultivate the habit of making timely decisions. You must conduct your due diligence and then trust your instincts. Making good decisions, timed right, is a significant challenge for any organization. Organizations in motion can alter course much faster than those that are stuck in one place. Decisions create momentum.

At Applied Materials, we used to envision ourselves standing on a cliff. One of three things could happen:

1. You give a correct answer to the question, and you stay on the cliff.

2. The wrong answer — you're pushed off.

3. No answer — you're also pushed off!

This scenario helps sharpen the mind. Within someone's area of responsibility, most people will give the right answer most of the time. They just need to decide. Then the team can move forward with whatever is necessary to do "the whole job" — complete the project, hire the person, or secure the donation.

Implementation is in part an attitude: Just do it. That perspective shows a bias toward action and thoughtful completion. Success is only 10 percent strategy. It's 90 percent implementation.

The Cost of Perfect Information

Voltaire said, "Don't let the perfect be the enemy of the good." That's sound advice. Time is wasted and opportunities are lost when people become fixated on having perfect information, rather than appreciating that there will never be enough information, nor will there be perfect decisions. That does not mean you agree to pursue long shots or ignore troubling data just to make sure you do something. You always want solid information, whether it's about your client's demographics, your program outputs and outcomes, or your nonprofit's financial condition.

But often people neglect to establish benchmarks and contingency plans and to do an honest assessment of whether the plan is working as the organization reaches (or doesn't reach) those key milestones. There will always be unexpected twists that can sabotage the best-laid plans, so having a Plan B at the ready is a sound practice. Once in motion, be prepared to adjust and recalibrate to ensure success.

At Applied Materials, we developed some ways of talking about this that empowered our people to keep moving forward at all times, even when it was difficult to predict what the competition would do, or where the economy might go, or whether we could meet an ambitious goal. Given the choice between waiting for complete information and riding momentum, I will take momentum every time.

Clear and proper communication by leadership is the first step in transitioning from decision-making to implementation. Make sure that people are clear on what the big decisions are and the rationale for them — even put them in writing to avoid misinterpretation. Be inclusive by disseminating them to the entire organization. The goal is to have your team gain a greater understanding of each decision, how it was made and by whom, thereby reducing your implementation risk.

Leading a nonprofit demands passion, perseverance, the ability to make decisions and communicate them, and to manage the consequences. When all is said and done, you don't want to be on the side of more was said than done. "Book it and ship it!"

Conversation Starters

For Chief Executives

1. How much time do you spend focused on your team's implementation work versus their strategy development? How do you promote the need to move ideas and action plans forward?

2. How comfortable are you with not having perfect information when making decisions? How does that impact your ability to take risks?

For Staff Team Members

1. What slows down or blocks your ability to make decisions?

2. How do you manage the consequences of decisions that have been made, monitoring them once in action? How do you assess whether course corrections are needed?

For Board Members

1. What processes and systems are in place to monitor the implementation of the board's earlier decisions and actions?

2. What is your tolerance for not having "perfect information" to inform the board's decision-making?

For Individual Donors

1. How do you go about assessing whether a nonprofit is successfully implementing its strategic plan? What additional tools or information can you use?

2. What specific types of information do you value and reference when considering where to make a donation or to volunteer your time?

For Institutional Philanthropies

1. When considering grant requests, what emphasis do you put on a nonprofit's projected plan versus its implementation of past plans?

2. How does the quest for perfect information impede your ability to work efficiently with grantees? How can you control risk without perfect information?

8

Who Owns the Monkey?

To create a culture of accountability,
reinforce individual ownership of problems.
Always ask, "Who owns the monkey?"

Nonprofit leaders are often overworked and under-resourced. As a result, staff problems can easily move up the chain of command. You need to create a culture of accountability to ensure that the only issues that land on your plate are the ones for which you hold clear responsibility.

Let's say that one of your staff shows up in your office with a problem — a monkey — on their shoulder. As a manager, you want to acknowledge that you see the monkey and that you care about the monkey. You may even feed the monkey for a few minutes. But you can't let that employee leave the monkey behind for you to take care of. Be sure that when they walk out the door of your office, the monkey goes too.

Owning the monkey means the person responsible cannot pass the buck; they must think through the consequences of decisions and try to solve the problems that arise.

Ask yourself, "Who owns the monkey?" Create an accountable culture; don't accept a victim mindset. If you set an example of taking responsibility for your own decisions, your people will do the same.

Empowerment

The notion of owning the monkey appeared in a Harvard Business Review article back in 1974, "Management Time: Who's Got the Monkey?" by William Oncken, Jr. and Donald L. Wass. They describe five degrees of initiatives that can empower staff decision-making. The employee could:

1. Wait until told (the lowest initiative).

2. Ask what to do.

3. Recommend an action and wait for a decision.

4. Act but inform at once.

5. Act, then report on the decision in due course (the highest initiative).

The manager's job is to outlaw the use of 1 and 2, and to ensure that for each problem leaving their office, there is an agreed-upon level of initiative assigned to it.

As management guru Stephen Covey points out in talking about monkeys, you should keep in mind that empowerment means you have to develop your staff's skills — a valuable investment. Managers should thoughtfully plan for an employee's development — with their input. Determine the right level of coaching and feedback for each direct report while avoiding micromanaging. You can reassure them that they have the skills and experience to make important decisions. Motivating your team members will boost their confidence and reassure them that they can take risks safely. My idea of management is serving as "First Assistant To" others, helping them to succeed.

Organizational Structure

The job of a chief executive is to create an organizational structure with functional processes. When the number of staff exceeds a few, if everybody in the nonprofit is reporting to the top executive, dysfunction is inevitable. A good leader needs to be able to communicate that in a growing organization, hierarchy is a good thing. It speeds up decision-making.

As a nonprofit shifts to a more hierarchical structure during a growth phase, leaders and managers need to determine who's responsible for each type of decision at every level; and that there is a structure that enables decentralized decision-making. You tune the structure and process to fit the work and the people and then urge your employees to make and take responsibility for their decisions. People will make mistakes, but you must make sure they own the monkey. If you step in and fix things for them, or punish them for reporting a problem, they will not make decisions.

In a culture of accountability, employees are more comfortable acknowledging reality, warts and all. Individuals do not just wait for someone else to solve the problem or hope things improve or spend their time crafting excuses or pointing fingers at others. They take responsibility for finding solutions and improvements for the problems over which they have clear authority.

At Applied Materials, people who owned their work, both its successes and failures, knew that we could adjust to an honest mistake. If people fail and do not learn though, you must move on and make changes fairly and quickly. Doing so, in fact, is respectful to your good performers who deserve to be surrounded and supported by competence and, ideally, excellence.

Conversation Starters

For Chief Executives

1. How can you serve as "First Assistant To" your staff, supporting them through successes and failures?

2. How does your organizational structure enable decentralized decision-making and empower staff to make and take responsibility for their decisions?

For Staff Team Members

1. Think of an instance where you dropped the monkey and your manager had to step in. What would you do differently next time?

2. In what ways do you see your chief executive and colleagues taking responsibility for their decisions? What can you learn from their examples?

For Board Members

1. What monkeys do you have responsibility for, separate from management's? What leadership skills are required to effectively own those monkeys?

2. How does the board communicate its accountability to stakeholders and the public?

For Individual Donors

1. In what ways can a nonprofit best demonstrate to you its accountability and transparency?

2. What does it take for a nonprofit to earn and maintain your trust and support?

For Institutional Philanthropies

1. How do your grantees demonstrate a culture of accountability and transparency? What would you do if you lose trust in a grantee?

2. Are your grant reporting requirements creating unnecessary work and taking time away from your grantees' focus on mission delivery? What could you do to simplify your requirements to be mutually beneficial to your institution and your grantees?

Applying Your Wisdom

Leadership and learning are indispensable to each other. — John F. Kennedy

Whatever your role or job title, you can improve your management skills with understanding and practice. I've found that a key to achieving success in work and life is to be a continuous learner. Collecting the management tips and insights in this booklet helped me evolve as a leader and manager. I've also become a better board member, volunteer, donor, foundation trustee, and even family man.

I encourage you to start your own collection of management ideas and catchphrases too. It will help shape and support your management style and your identity as a leader.

Take Action

Now that you have read this booklet, you may be asking yourself: where should I go from here? Perhaps you've discovered some new ideas that you think can be helpful or have been reminded of an older concept that now applies to a current situation. But it's not enough just to read about management development. I hope that you are inspired to take action. Remember, success is 90 percent implementation!

To continue your Applied Wisdom journey, visit **AppliedWisdomforNonprofits.org** where you can download the ebook or audiobook version. You'll also find a five-minute online self-assessment and practical downloadable tools (videos, templates, slide presentations and more). These were created for your use — for organizations with their staff and board teams, for donors with their favorite nonprofit leaders, and for field builders in their training and coaching.

Organizational Capacity Building

For any organization, this booklet can be used as a capacity-building tool and culture-change framework. Consider leveraging this booklet as the cornerstone of your organization's learning and development program. Provide equal opportunity to everyone to develop themselves individually and collaboratively as part of a team. Set up a book club where people read and reflect on a particular insight. Tackle some of the "Conversation Starters" questions by integrating them into monthly staff or board meetings. Build in an accountability element to move your people forward and achieve optimal results. Creating these types of engaging learning opportunities will build team cohesion, and empower individuals to improve their leadership skills, regardless of their title or position.

Whether you self-direct these activities or engage a consultant, positively transforming the behavior and habits of your people will enhance their professional growth and impact your nonprofit's ability to deliver greater outcomes.

Be a continuous learner — join our learning community at **AppliedWisdomforNonprofits.org**.

To your success,

Jim Morgan

About James C. Morgan

James C. Morgan is often referred to as a "bridge builder" between business and the nonprofit and philanthropy sectors. He is respected for his transformational management style that inspires and empowers people to achieve excellence and become outstanding managers and leaders.

Jim is one of the most influential nonprofit and philanthropic leaders in Silicon Valley. Possessing a rare blend of technological aptitude, business acumen, and leadership skills, he advanced the semiconductor industry worldwide. Jim led the semiconductor equipment giant, Applied Materials, for nearly three decades — one of the longest tenures of any Fortune 500 CEO.

Under his leadership, Applied Materials received numerous awards for its commitment to achieving sustainability and for its socially responsible practices. Industry Week named Applied Materials one of America's Best Managed Companies and Fortune magazine selected it as one of America's 100 Best Companies to Work For, and among the Best Companies for Minorities.

Nonprofit and Philanthropic Contributions

As co-founder of The Northern Sierra Partnership, Jim spurred the formation of a pioneering collaboration by bringing five conservation nonprofits together to do what none could do alone. The partnership has successfully preserved over 90,000 acres in the California Sierra Nevada Mountains. Jim also volunteers as a fundraising campaign chair and has helped raise more than $200 million for conservation efforts in Northern California.

Jim served as both a California and global trustee, as well as co-chair of the Asia Pacific Council of The Nature Conservancy (TNC), a worldwide nonprofit that focuses on programs that "Protect Nature and Preserve Life." He was honored with The Nature Conservancy's prestigious Oak Leaf Award.

In 1993, Jim co-founded, along with his wife Becky Morgan, a former California State Senator, the Morgan Family Foundation. Their shared goal is to change lives and transform communities. They like to "give forward," to help individuals and organizations reach their full potential.

Jim also served as an advisory board member for Santa Clara University's Miller Center for Social Entrepreneurship, the largest and most successful university-based social enterprise accelerator in the world.

Recognition and Awards

Jim has served as a technology adviser to three U.S. presidents, including George H. W. Bush and George W. Bush. In 1996, he was presented with the National Medal of Technology and Innovation by President Bill Clinton.

He was instrumental in creating The Tech Interactive's Tech for Global Good awards and inspired the James C. Morgan Global Humanitarian Award, honoring individuals whose broad vision and leadership are focused on combating critical global problems. Past recipients have included Bill Gates, Gordon Moore, Al Gore, and Julie Packard.

Among Jim's many honors are the Global Semiconductor Association Dr. Morris Chang Award; SIA and IEEE Robert N. Noyce Awards; the Silicon Valley Leadership Group Lifetime Achievement Award; The Tech Interactive Global Humanitarian Award; and the National Fish and Wildlife Foundation Award.

Jim and Becky have been married for more than 50 years. They reside in Northern California near their two children and five grandchildren.

About Diane Parnes

Diane Parnes is an inspirational consultant and trusted social impact advisor empowering mission-driven CEOs, staff, and board leaders to create positive change and transformation. Based in Silicon Valley, she advises and coaches nonprofits and foundations nationwide.

Diane has spent her entire 30-year career starting up and scaling nonprofits and advising ultra-high net worth philanthropists. Her career started as a certified fundraising executive and evolved into executive director roles at two Bay Area nonprofits. Ultimately recruited to the philanthropic world, she became a high-tech global grantmaker followed by 20 years of service as chief executive of several major Silicon Valley foundations. During her leadership of the Sobrato Family Foundation, she and the foundation were recognized by the National Association of Fundraising Professionals with the Outstanding Foundation Award, both nationally and by the Silicon Valley Chapter.

For the last two decades, Diane has been a sector leader and champion of unrestricted, multi-year general operating support and organizational capacity-building initiatives with an emphasis on strengthening staff leaders and board governance. All of her individual and foundation clients have adopted that strategic giving approach based on her recommendation. She's directed hundreds of millions of dollars for community benefit through cash giving, rent-free office and meeting space grants, and technology equipment grants, affordable housing loans and other special initiatives.

Diane has been recognized as a Silicon Valley "Woman of Influence" and honored for her volunteer service by the Association of Fundraising Professionals – Silicon Valley chapter. She is a past board chair of Northern California Grantmakers, CompassPoint Nonprofit Services and Association of Fundraising Professionals – Silicon Valley. Her twelve other board roles include a nonprofit public policy and advocacy group, venture philanthropy fund, community foundation, and numerous philanthropy field-building associations. She is an active presenter/moderator at sector conferences and convenings and has been cited in regional and national philanthropy publications.

Join our learning community at
AppliedWisdomforNonprofits.org

Read

Booklet in digital or print format,
ideal for distributing or mailing to board members or donors.

Listen

Audiobook to listen to on your daily commute or walk.

Watch

Short videos for staff, board, volunteer and donor meetings.

Tools & Resources

Downloadable learning tools and resources
to implement Applied Wisdom effectively.

NOTES